D1080371

THE PENNYWISE COOKBOOK

by Lorna Walker

Produced for the Dairy Industry

The author would like to thank the following for
their co-operation in supplying accessories for use
in the photographs:

Elizabeth David, 46 Bourne Street, London SW1
Casa Pupo, 56 Pimlico Road, London SW1
Robert Carrier Cookshop, 80/82 Pimlico Road,
London SW1.
Dairy Produce Advisory Service, Milk Marketing Board,
Thames Ditton, Surrey.

Photography by ROGER TUFF
Printed by Sir Joseph Causton & Sons Limited
ISBN 0 903438 01 1

Index to Recipes

THE PENNYWISE COOKBOOK

The 'pennywise' cook knows how to make the most of her weekly budget by choosing food carefully and presenting it attractively. Although it is said 'if you look after the pennies the pounds look after themselves', in this decimal age I'm not so sure that they do look after themselves. So here is a book of penny-wise recipes aimed at making the most of the weekly budget.

Budget cooking usually means buying the cheaper cuts of meat and cooking for a longer time to make them tender, but for many to be pennywise means being timewise as well. If you have an outside job, your time for cooking in the home is limited and because of this you may find yourself buying the more expensive cuts of meat that take a shorter time to cook, so you will find recipes included which are quick to make and at the same time reasonable in cost. I have also included recipes using 'convenience' foods which, although not strictly budgetwise, do cut down on preparation time but, if you prefer, you can always substitute the fresh or home-made version instead of the can or packet.

There will be different views and reasons within your own family on what is sensible spending. It is, therefore, worth while looking at a few basic points that help food budgeting to see how these may be applied to your own requirements.

1 Planning in advance

Haphazard day-to-day planning of menus is all very well, but it is not the most economical way of setting about things. The most sensible way of doing it is to sit down and plan meals for the week. The menus can be so planned that it is only necessary to shop about twice a week and with a couple of big cooking sessions a week, too. Maximum advantage can then be taken of oven planning by deciding on a number of items that can be cooked at the same time to use all the oven space and heat. Planning in advance also means that if you read or listen to shopping information (well worth while!) you can then incorporate it into the week's menus.

2 Shopping sensibly

Having planned the week's menus in advance, this also helps to speed up shopping. Instead of wandering around trying to get inspiration, all you have to do is make a list of the ingredients for the meals and buy those items not in store, thus giving more time to look around and find the best value for money. Another sensible way to shop, if you have the time, is to first have a good look at what the shops have on display, then base your menus on the best buys.

Shopping at a market where the prices are more competitive and the food always fresh (because they have not got the facilities for storage) is invariably good but, remember, travelling a distance to go to a market or cheaper shop is not worth while unless you are going to save more than the cost of your journey!

3 Storing food

Having shopped economically it would be a waste of time and money to store the food badly.

Dairy foods: All dairy foods should be stored in a cold larder o refrigerator and used in rotation.

Milk stored in a jug in a refrigerator should be covered to avoid tainting by other foods (self-sealing plastic film is good for this). Do not mix two lots of milk of different ages (unless to be used immediately) as the older milk will age the fresh milk.

Cheeses keep very well if wrapped individually and stored in a folded polythene bag in the refrigerator or cold larder, but for best flavour bring to room temperature about one hour before serving.

Butter, once removed from its wrapper, should be kept in a covered container in a refrigerator or cold larder, but it's a good idea to keep some at room temperature so that it's ready for immediate use.

Meat, poultry and fish: Always remove shop wrappings. Loosely cover (muslin is good) and store in a cold airy place or coldest shelf in a refrigerator.

Most meat properly stored will keep for 3–4 days. Mince or offal will keep 1–2 days and sliced bacon will keep for about a week. Fish should be eaten within 24 hours of purchase.

Vegetables and fruit: Root vegetables are best stored in a dark, airy place.

Green vegetables are best kept in open polythene bags in a cold place.

Nearly all fruit keeps longer if kept cold—bananas should not be stored in a refrigerator, only because their skins will discolour.

Frozen foods: Follow pack instructions for storage, and never re-freeze once thawed.

4 Bulk buying

Both time and money can be saved by buying in bulk. This can be done through a discount store cash-and-carry warehouse or even through some local grocers who will offer discount on quantity purchases. Before deciding to bulk-buy, there are certain considerations that you should make to ensure it will be worth while.

a Is the discount substantial enough for you to give up storage space, or could you buy the items freshly, as required, at a competitive grocer for more or less the same price?

b Have you the space to keep large packs in good condition?

c Will your budget allow a large amount to be bought at one time?

d Remember that many items have a limited storage life and the family may tire of eating the same thing too frequently. It is a help you can find someone to share the buying with you,to gain the advantage of the lower prices without having to deal with the quantity.

e It's very easy to be extravagant with something of which you have a lot!

5 Use of convenience equipment

a Home freezer: If you consider that you will save money and time, the capital outlay and high running costs will be justified. A home freezer is a good method of gaining the advantages of bulk purchase. In addition, foods can be bought at the height of the season when they are at their best . . . and cheapest. With a freezer you can bulk cook when you have the time and use it when time is at a premium.

In addition, you are much more likely to use up the little bits and pieces that are left over after a roast lunch. For instance, a few roast potatoes, greens, and gravy . . . put in a foil tray with some sliced meat means that on a future date you have a ready-made dinner for one.

With a few exceptions (mainly salad vegetables) most foods freeze well, but before buying a large quantity it is important to check how long it can be stored without deterioration.

Freezing dairy products

Butter may be frozen up to three months, but when taken from the freezer it needs to be used up a little quicker than fresh butter.

Milk: Homogenised milk in waxed cartons freezes well for about a month.

Cheese freezes well, wrapped in foil for up to four months.

Cream: Whipping or double cream may be frozen, lightly whipped (with or without sugar) for three months. It's a good idea to freeze it in single-portion whirls ready to pop on the top of desserts. It does need to be used soon after it has thawed.

b Electric mixer: A mixer can save money if it encourages you to regularly make cakes and pastries instead of buying them.
A good cook will argue that she gets better volume (and quantity when mixing cakes and meringues, etc, by hand . . . but she will take longer and feel more fatigued. Besides, for the not-so-good cook, a mixer lessens the risk of a failure!

c Liquidiser: Like other electrical appliances a liquidiser is on worth while when used to the full. It is particularly good for baby foods and soups (a few left-over cooked vegetables, a stock cube and some milk blended together can make the most delicious soup). Drinks can be made with fresh oranges or lemons (so much better than the very sweet, often synthetic bottled fruit drinks) or by blending fruits or flavours into milk . . . very useful for persuading difficult children to take milk which is so essential for their health.

6 A healthy family
A balanced diet is essential for the good health of your family and growth of your children. It is, therefore, particularly important when trying to cut down the cost of the weekly food budget that you do not cut down on the nutritive value of the food.

Each member of the family should, every day, eat or drink: on pint of milk, a portion of meat or fish or cheese, or eggs plus vegetables, fruit, bread and butter. If you are cutting down food because you are slimming, it is very important to make sure that you eat sufficient of the right foods to keep your body in good health.

7 Metrication
As metrication gradually takes over, you may wish to convert some of these recipes to metric measures. It is generally accepted that the most convenient way to do this is to take 25 grammes as 1 ounce.

Grammes	Approximate Conversion	Rounded Figur
25 g	0.9 oz	1 oz
50 g	1.75 oz	2 oz
100 g	3.5 oz	3 oz
200 g	7.0 oz	6 oz
250 g	9.0 oz	8 oz
500 g	17.5 oz	16 oz (1 lb)
1000 g (1 Kg)	2.2 lb	32 oz (2 lb)

STARTERS AND MAIN COURSES

1. Corn Chowder—Page 15
2. Leicester Baked Fish—Page 17
3. Nutty Chicken—Page 33
4. Canneloni—Page 41
5. Savoury Cocottes—Page 14

9

Smoked Fish Pâté

Serves 4

3 large smoked kipper fillets (cooked)
6 oz (approximately) home-produced butter
Pepper
Juice of ½ lemon
Parsley and lemon slices

1 Remove skin and bone from kipper fillets.
2 Place flesh in a bowl with half its weight in butter.
Add pepper. Mash together until they are so well
blended that a smooth paste is formed.
3 Mix in lemon juice.
4 Spoon the pâté into 4 individual dishes and chill
before serving. Garnish each with a sprig of parsley and
a thin slice of lemon.

Smoked Fish Pâté is good served with crisp Melba
toast which you can either buy or make yourself—
cut *very* thin slices of brown bread, remove crusts,
then cook the slices in a moderate oven until they are
crisp and beginning to brown.

Country Pâté

Serves 4

5-6 rashers streaky bacon
½ oz flour
½ oz home-produced butter
¼ pint milk
4 oz belly pork
4 oz pig's liver
1 oz onion
4 oz sausage meat
1 clove garlic (finely chopped or crushed)
2 tablespoons dry sherry or brandy (optional)
Salt and pepper
1 bay leaf

1 Remove rind from streaky bacon. Flatten each rasher with blade of a knife, then use to line a 1-pint pâté mould or loaf tin.
2 Place the flour, butter and milk in a saucepan; heat, whisking continuously, until sauce thickens.
3 Mince the pork, liver, onion and sausage meat together twice and add to the sauce. Stir in the garlic and sherry. Season to taste with salt and pepper.
4 Turn the pâté mixture into the lined mould. Top with a bay leaf. Cover with a lid or aluminium foil. Stand in a roasting tin half filled with water. Bake—mark 4, 350°F, for 1 hour.
5 Let the pâté become cold in the tin before turning out, then leave for a day or overnight in a cold place for flavours to develop. Serve sliced with hot toast and a bowl of radishes or pieces of celery.

Timewise pâté—for a very quick smooth pâté, fry 1 lb chicken livers in 3 oz butter just until the blood starts running. Then liquidise or sieve the pan contents. Stir in two tablespoons cream, the same amount of brandy and season to taste. Leave until cold, then spoon individual portions on to a lettuce leaf and eat with hot toast.

Cream of Watercress Soup

Serves 6

2 bunches watercress
2 oz home-produced butter
3 oz onions (finely chopped)
1½ pints milk
1½ level tablespoons flour
2 chicken stock cubes
2 tablespoons fresh cream (optional)

1 Wash the watercress, then coarsely chop, and remove any thick stalks.
2 Melt the butter. Add the watercress and onions and cook gently for 5-6 minutes.
3 Boil the milk.
4 Stir the flour, stock cubes and boiling milk on to the watercress and onions. Cover and simmer for 15-20 minutes.
5 Pass the soup through a fine sieve (or liquidise). Reheat and serve, spooning, if liked, a little cream and some croûtons on each portion.

   To make croûtons, cut bread into small cubes and toss with butter and a little salt, over a fairly high heat until crisp and golden.

Unusual Vegetable Soup

Serves 4-5

1 (4 oz) packet frozen mixed vegetables
1 beef stock cube
$\frac{3}{4}$ pint water
1 (5 fl oz) carton natural yogurt
1 egg yolk
Lemon rind (finely grated)
Mint (finely chopped)

1 Place the mixed vegetables, stock cube and water in
a saucepan. Slowly bring to the boil and simmer for
10 minutes.
2 Mix the yogurt with the egg yolk. Stir in some of the
hot soup, then whisk this mixture back into the
remaining hot soup. Keep stirring while soup is reheated.
3 Serve the soup topped with finely grated lemon rind
and chopped mint leaves.
   This soup is based on a Greek recipe and has rather
a distinctive flavour.

Parmentier Soup

Serves 6

2 oz home-produced butter
3 oz onions (thinly sliced)
1 lb potatoes (peeled and thinly sliced)
1 bay leaf
2 chicken stock cubes
1 pint milk
$\frac{1}{2}$ pint water
Chopped chives
2 oz Scottish Cheddar cheese (grated)

1 Melt the butter in a heavy saucepan. Add the onions
and potatoes. Cover and cook slowly for about
5 minutes.
2 Add the bay leaf, stock cubes, milk and water.
Cover and continue to cook slowly for 30 minutes.
3 Pass the soup through a fine sieve (or liquidise), to
form a purée.
4 Serve the soup sprinkled with chopped chives and
grated cheese.

Savoury Cocottes

Serves 4

1 (4 oz) carton cottage cheese
$\frac{1}{4}$ pint milk
1 egg
2 oz liver sausage (finely chopped)
$\frac{1}{4}$ level teaspoon mixed dried herbs
Salt and pepper
$\frac{1}{2}$ oz home-produced butter
1 tomato
Parsley

1 Preheat the oven, mark 6, 400°F.
2 Beat the cottage cheese, milk and egg together, stir in the chopped liver sausage and mixed herbs. Season to taste with salt and pepper.
3 Spoon the savoury mixture into 4 individual buttered heatproof dishes and bake for 10-15 minutes.
4 Garnish each with a slice of tomato and sprig of parsley.

Mushroom Hors d'oeuvre

Serves 4-6

8 oz button mushrooms (sliced)
2 (5 fl oz) cartons natural yogurt
1 tablespoon lemon juice
$\frac{1}{2}$ clove garlic (finely crushed)
2 tablespoons parsley (chopped)
1 tablespoon chives (chopped)
Salt and pepper
1 lettuce (washed)

1 Combine all ingredients except lettuce. Season to taste.
2 Leave mushrooms to marinate for at least 4 hours before serving.
3 Serve Mushroom Hors d'oeuvre on a bed of lettuce.

Corn Chowder

Serves 6

1 green pepper (core and seeds removed)
4 oz streaky bacon (shredded)
4 oz onions (chopped)
1 stick celery (chopped)
6 oz potatoes (peeled and diced)
1 bay leaf
1 teaspoon grated nutmeg
$\frac{3}{4}$ pint water
Salt and pepper
1 oz flour
1 pint milk
1 (11$\frac{1}{2}$ oz) can sweetcorn (drained)
Chopped parsley

1 Chop the green pepper finely and cook in boiling salted water for 3 minutes. Drain and place aside.
2 Fry the bacon gently until just brown, then add the chopped onions and celery and continue frying until golden brown.
3 Add the green pepper, potato, bay leaf, nutmeg, water, salt and pepper to the browned vegetables and bacon. Bring to the boil, then simmer slowly until the potatoes are soft.
4 Blend the flour with a little of the milk to make a smooth liquid. Stir it into the soup with the remaining milk and sweetcorn. Continue stirring until the soup comes to the boil.
5 Serve the chowder thickly dusted with chopped parsley.

A chowder is a thick soup, usually milk based, containing diced potatoes and bacon. With the addition of sweetcorn or clams, chowders are favourites in the USA, the country where this version originated. It is a delicious, filling soup that is almost a meal in itself and, if served as a first course, should only be followed by something quite light.

Mock Scampi with Tartare Sauce

Serves 4

1 lb whiting (or plaice) fillets (skinned)
Flour
Salt and pepper
Beaten egg
Golden breadcrumbs
1 rounded teaspoon capers (finely chopped)
1 rounded teaspoon gherkins (finely chopped)
1 rounded teaspoon onion (finely chopped)
1 rounded teaspoon parsley (finely chopped)
$\frac{1}{4}$ pint thick mayonnaise
Fresh cream or milk
Deep fat for frying
Lemon wedges

1 Cut the fillets of fish into strips 2 inches × $\frac{1}{2}$ inch wide.
2 Toss the fish strips in seasoned flour. Brush them with beaten egg and coat with breadcrumbs.
3 Tartare Sauce: Mix the chopped capers, gherkins, onion and parsley into the mayonnaise and thin it down with a little cream or milk. Leave to one side.
4 Heat the deep fat until there is a faint haze, then fry the mock scampi until crisp and golden (about 5 minutes).
5 Pile the fish on to a hot dish. Garnish with lemon wedges and serve with Tartare Sauce.

Leicester Baked Fish

Serves 6

4 oz streaky bacon
2 oz onions (chopped)
4 oz mushrooms (chopped)
2½ oz home-produced butter
4 oz fresh breadcrumbs
¾ pint milk
Salt and pepper
2 (¾ lb) fillets of cod
4 oz Leicester cheese (grated)
2 oz flour
2 tomatoes (sliced)
Chopped parsley

1 Mince or chop the bacon. Fry the bacon, onions and
mushrooms in 1 oz of the butter until tender. Stir in the
breadcrumbs and bind the stuffing with a little milk.
Season to taste.
2 Remove skin from fish. Place one of the fillets in a
heatproof dish and spoon over the stuffing. Place the
other fillet on top.
3 Place 3 oz of the grated cheese, remaining butter,
½ pint milk and flour in a saucepan; heat, whisking
continuously, until sauce thickens. Season to taste and
pour over fish to coat.
4 Arrange the sliced tomatoes on top of the fish and
sprinkle with remaining cheese. Bake—mark 4, 350°F,
for about 40 minutes.
5 Sprinkle fish with chopped parsley and cut it into
thick slices to serve

   I happen to like the flavour and colour of Leicester
cheese with fish, but this dish can be made equally
well with Scottish cheeses—only don't forget to
change the title.

Russian Fish Pie

Serves 4

1 lb cod or haddock fillet (skinned)
$1\frac{1}{2}$ oz home-produced butter
Lemon juice
Salt and pepper
1 oz flour
$\frac{1}{4}$ pint milk
1 (13 oz) packet frozen puff pastry (thawed)
Beaten egg

1. Place the fish, with $\frac{1}{2}$ oz of the butter, squeeze of lemon juice, salt and pepper between 2 large plates. Cook over pan of boiling water for 15-20 minutes.
2 Place the flour, remaining butter and milk in a saucepan; heat, whisking continuously, until the sauce thickens.
3 Remove bones, flake the fish, and fold it into the sauce. Season to taste with salt and pepper.
4 Roll out the pastry to a square 12 inches × 12 inches. Place the fish sauce in the middle. Bring each corner of pastry into the centre and seal along the edges with water to make a square pastry envelope.
5 Brush the top of the pie with beaten egg. Bake— mark 7, 425°F, for 30-40 minutes.

Timewise tip: Putting all the white sauce ingredients in the pan together (see stage 2) is really much quicker and easier than the conventional method. To save time, try it whenever you need a white sauce—for best results use a looped wire sauce whisk.

A good variation to Russian Fish Pie is either the addition of chopped hard-boiled egg and finely chopped gherkin or grated cheese. With pies that have pastry on top and a thick sauce filling, it is unnecessary to serve potatoes. Try serving with beans and carrots.

Swedish Herring Salad

Serves 4

4 roll-mop herrings
1 dessert apple (peeled and diced)
2 oz onions (finely chopped)
$\frac{1}{2}$ lb cold cooked potato (diced)
2 oz pickled cucumber (diced)
2 (5 fl oz) cartons natural yogurt
2 hard-boiled eggs
4 oz cooked beetroot (diced)
Chopped parsley

1 Shred the herrings; place in a bowl with the apple,
onions, potato and pickled cucumber. Add the yogurt
and stir together. Turn into a serving dish.
2 Slice the hard-boiled eggs and arrange in rows
alternating with the diced beetroot and parsley.

Sea Pie

Serves 4-6

1 lb cod fillet (skinned)
3 oz onions (very thinly sliced)
Salt and pepper
1 bay leaf
Juice of $\frac{1}{2}$ lemon
$\frac{1}{4}$ pint water
4 oz mushrooms (sliced)
$2\frac{1}{2}$ oz home-produced butter
1 (2-4 oz) can mussels (optional)
$1\frac{1}{2}$ oz plain flour
$\frac{3}{4}$ pint milk
4 oz self-raising flour
1 level teaspoon mixed dried herbs

1 Skin the fish and cut into large chunks. Place in an ovenproof dish. Add the onion, salt, pepper, bay leaf, lemon juice and $\frac{1}{4}$ pint water. Cover the fish with foil. Bake—mark 5, 375°F, for approximately 20 minutes until fish is tender.
2 Lift the cooked fish out with a draining spoon and place it in a 3-pint pie dish. Reserve the stock, but discard bay leaf.
3 Slowly fry the sliced mushrooms in a saucepan in $\frac{1}{2}$ oz of the butter until tender. Lift them out with the draining spoon and add them to the fish with the drained mussels.
4 Add 1 oz butter to the saucepan in which the mushrooms were cooked, together with the plain flour, $\frac{1}{2}$ pint of the milk and the reserved fish stock. Whisk over a medium heat until sauce thickens. Adjust seasoning to taste and pour over the fish.
5 Rub the remaining 1 oz butter into the self-raising flour. Add the mixed herbs, salt and pepper. Stir in sufficient milk (about $\frac{1}{4}$ pint) to make a soft but not sticky scone dough.
6 Lightly pat or roll the dough out to fit the top of the pic dish. Cut it almost through into 4-6 sections. Brush with milk. Bake—mark 8, 450°F, for 10 minutes, then reduce heat to mark 3, 325°F, and cook for a further 15-20 minutes until scone dough is cooked through.

With the herbed scone topping—potatoes are not necessary. Serve with baked tomatoes and peas.

Curried Haddock

Serves 6

1½ lb haddock fillet
3 oz onions (finely chopped)
1 clove garlic (finely chopped)
2 oz home-produced butter
1 small dessert apple (chopped)
2 cloves
1 level tablespoon curry powder
4 level teaspoons flour
½ pint milk
½ pint stock (may be made from a chicken stock cube)
4 oz tomatoes (skinned and chopped)
1 oz sultanas
2 level teaspoons tomato purée
2 level tablespoons sweet chutney
1 piece stem ginger (chopped)
Salt and pepper
4-6 oz long-grain rice (cooked)
Lemon wedges

1 Remove skin and cut fish into 1-inch squares.
2 Fry onions and garlic gently in the butter for about
5 minutes. Add the apple and cloves, then continue
cooking for a few minutes. Stir in the curry powder and
cook for 2 minutes, then stir in the flour and cook for a
further 2 minutes.
3 Remove the pan from the heat. Stir in the milk and
stock, then, stirring continuously, bring to the boil and
cook until the sauce thickens.
4 Add the chopped tomatoes, sultanas, tomato purée,
chutney, chopped ginger, salt and pepper. Cover and
cook gently for 10 minutes. Stir in the fish and
cook for a further 10-15 minutes until the fish is tender.
5 Check seasoning of curry and serve with the rice,
garnished with lemon wedges.

A good way to use up cold cooked chicken is to make
this same sauce and add chopped chicken instead of
fish at stage 4.

Tuna Croquettes
with Mushroom Sauce

Serves 2-4

1 oz flour
1 oz home-produced butter
$\frac{1}{4}$ pint milk
1 ($6\frac{1}{2}$ oz) can tuna fish
4 gherkins
Salt and pepper
1 egg (beaten)
1 oz golden breadcrumbs
Deep fat for frying
1 ($10\frac{1}{2}$ oz) can condensed cream of mushroom soup
4 slices of fried bread

1 Place flour, butter and milk in a saucepan, heat, whisking continuously, until the sauce thickens.
2 Flake the tuna fish and add two of the gherkins, finely chopped. Fold into the sauce. Season to taste with salt and pepper.
3 Divide into four equal portions. Shape into round cakes, using floured hands. Dip in beaten egg and coat in crumbs. Place in refrigerator or cool place for $\frac{1}{2}$ hour.
4 Fry in deep fat until golden brown. Drain.
5 Meanwhile, blend the soup with only $\frac{1}{2}$ can of water and heat to almost boiling point.
6 Serve each croquette on a slice of fried bread, garnished with a slice of gherkin. Serve the sauce separately.

If you are not being too 'pennywise' these croquettes are very good made with salmon instead of tuna— and it is one way of making salmon go a long way.

Mackerel Baked with Yogurt and Cream

Serves 4

4 medium-size mackerel
1 (5 fl oz) carton natural yogurt
4 tablespoons fresh double cream
Salt and pepper
Lemon wedges
Watercress

1 Preheat the oven, mark 5, 375°F.
2 Wash mackerel; dry them well and place them in an ovenproof dish.
3 Beat the yogurt and cream together. Season to taste and pour over the fish. Bake for 15-20 minutes until the fish is cooked through.
4 Serve garnished with lemon wedges and watercress.

Chicken and Ham Mousse

Serves 4-6

$\frac{1}{2}$ oz home-produced butter
$\frac{1}{2}$ oz flour
1 pint milk
$\frac{1}{2}$ oz gelatine
4 tablespoons hot water
Worcestershire sauce
Salt and pepper
1 (7 oz) can tomatoes (sieved)
6 oz chicken (minced)
6 oz ham (minced)
Cochineal

1 Place the butter, flour and milk in a saucepan; heat, whisking continuously, until the sauce is cooked and thickened. Cool.
2 Dissolve gelatine in hot water. Blend with the cooled white sauce and season well with Worcestershire sauce, salt and pepper.
3 Combine with the sieved tomatoes and the minced meats. Add a few drops of cochineal and pour into a wetted mould.
4 When set, turn out and serve with green salad.

Pennywise tip: Instead of buying the ham in slices for mincing, it's worth asking the grocer if he has any pieces or broken slices. These are often collected during a day and sold at a reduced price. This applies to most cold cooked meats. It's a great saving with something like smoked salmon which is delicious minced, seasoned with lemon juice and black pepper and piled on to thickly buttered brown bread fingers.

Chicken Kiev

Serves 4

1 good-size clove of garlic (optional)
1 level tablespoon parsley (finely chopped)
4 oz home-produced butter
Salt and pepper
4 chicken breasts (boned)
Beaten egg
Golden crumbs
Deep fat for frying

1 Crush or very finely chop the garlic and place it in a bowl with the parsley, butter, salt and pepper. Mash well together. Chill until firm.
2 Flatten each chicken breast with a rolling pin.
3 Divide the butter mixture into 4 and roll each into a sausage shape. Place one on each piece of chicken.
4 Wrap the chicken round the butter mixture to form firm 'parcels'. Either sew or tie in place with cotton (leaving long ends, so that threads can easily be removed later).
5 Dip the chicken 'parcels' into beaten egg, then golden crumbs—twice. Place aside to chill.
6 Heat the deep fat and fry the chicken parcels for 5 minutes. Remove threads. Serve immediately. Good with boiled rice and chopped spinach.

One of the most succulent and delicious of chicken dishes—if you are a garlic lover. Otherwise good with fresh chopped herbs mixed with the butter instead of garlic. To test if fat is hot enough for frying—a one-inch cube of bread should turn golden brown in one minute.

Honey Barbecued Chicken

Serves 4

2 oz home-produced butter
4 oz onions (finely chopped)
1 clove garlic (finely chopped) optional
1 (14 oz) can tomatoes
2 tablespoons Worcestershire sauce
1 tablespoon honey
Salt and pepper
4 oz long-grain rice
4 chicken drumsticks
Mushrooms ⎫
Tomatoes ⎬ to garnish
Watercress ⎭

1 Combine the butter, chopped onions, garlic, tomatoes, Worcestershire sauce, honey, plenty of salt and pepper, in a saucepan. Gently heat together for $\frac{1}{2}$ hour.
2 Cook the rice according to directions on the pack. Keep hot.
3 Place the chicken drumsticks in the grill pan and brush liberally with the barbecue sauce.
4 Grill the chicken for 10 minutes on each side, brushing frequently with more sauce.
5 Serve the barbecued chicken on a bed of rice garnished with grilled mushrooms, tomatoes and watercress. Serve remaining sauce separately.

When chestnuts are in season, I have served this barbecued chicken scattered with chestnuts, boiled then fried in butter until turning golden.

Monday Pie

Serves 4-5

$\frac{3}{4}$ lb cold roast beef
3 oz onions
1 ($6\frac{1}{2}$ oz) can tomatoes
1 ($7\frac{3}{4}$ oz) can baked beans
1 level teaspoon flour
1 level teaspoon gravy powder
Salt and pepper
1 lb potatoes
3 oz Scottish Cheddar cheese (grated)

1 Mince the cold roast beef and onions into a basin. Stir in the canned tomatoes, baked beans, flour, gravy powder, salt and pepper and turn into a $1\frac{1}{2}$-pint shallow pie dish.
2 Peel and slice the potatoes, arrange on top of the meat.
3 Bake—mark 5, 375°F, for approximately 40 minutes. 10 minutes before end of baking time, sprinkle with grated cheese.
   A good quick way of using up cold roast beef.

Nutty Chicken

Serves 4

1 (10 oz) can condensed mushroom soup
$\frac{1}{4}$ pint milk
8 oz cooked chicken (chopped)
5 oz long-grain rice (cooked)
4 oz mushrooms (chopped)
2 oz peanuts (shelled)
3 rashers streaky bacon (finely chopped)
2 oz Scottish Cheddar cheese (grated)

1 Mix the soup with the milk in a large bowl. Stir in the chicken, rice and mushrooms and turn into a $1\frac{1}{2}$-pint pie dish.
2 Coarsely chop the nuts and mix with the bacon and grated cheese, sprinkle over the pie.
3 Bake pie for 25 minutes, mark 6, 400°F, until topping is golden brown.
   Note: If this dish is to be served to young children do not include peanuts in the topping.

Quick Chick Casserole

Serves 4

4 chicken joints
4 oz onions (chopped)
1 ($10\frac{1}{2}$ oz) can condensed mushroom soup
$\frac{1}{4}$ pint milk
$\frac{1}{2}$ level teaspoon mixed dried herbs

1 Place the chicken joints in the casserole with the chopped onions.
2 Mix the condensed soup with the milk and herbs and spoon over the chicken.
3 Cover the casserole and bake—mark 4, 350°F, for $1\frac{1}{4}$ hours. Remove lid and continue cooking casserole for a further 15-20 minutes until the chicken is tender.

Timewise tip: When cooking casseroles, brush the dish with butter before putting in the meat—it will be much easier to wash up afterwards.

Beef Layer Pie
with Yogurt Topping

Serves 4

4 oz onions (chopped)
1 oz home-produced butter
$\frac{1}{2}$ lb cold roast beef (minced)
$\frac{1}{4}$ level teaspoon mixed herbs
2 level tablespoons tomato purée
1 teaspoon Worcestershire sauce
Salt and pepper
1 lb potatoes (cooked)
$\frac{1}{2}$ lb tomatoes (skinned and sliced)
1 egg
1 oz flour
1 (5 fl oz) carton natural yogurt
Paprika

1 Cook the onions gently in the butter. Add the cooked minced meat, mixed herbs, tomato purée and Worcestershire sauce. Season well to taste.
2 Starting with the potatoes, arrange layers of potato, then the meat mixture, then tomatoes into a 2-pint casserole, finishing with a layer of potatoes. Cover casserole. Bake—mark 5, 375°F, for 30 minutes.
3 Beat the egg and blend in the flour and the yogurt. Season to taste and spoon over the pie after it has cooked for 30 minutes.
4 Return pie with topping to the oven and cook for a further 30 minutes. Dust top with paprika before serving.

A good dish for using up cold meat—good with lamb or chicken, too!

Danish Meat Fritter-Cakes

Serves 8 (about 24 fritter-cakes)

½ lb stewing beef
½ lb pie pork
3 oz onions
4 oz plain flour
Salt and pepper
1 egg (beaten)
½ pint milk
Fat or oil for frying

1 Mince the beef, pork and onions together.
2 Sieve the flour, salt and pepper into a bowl.
Gradually blend in the beaten egg and milk to make a smooth batter.
3 Stir the minced meat mixture into the batter and leave aside for about ½ hour.
4 Slowly heat fat or oil, ¼-inch deep, in a frying pan.
5 Spoon rounded tablespoons of the mixture into the hot fat. Lower heat and fry fritter-cakes for approximately 15 minutes, turning them from time to time, until the batter is crisp and the meat is cooked through.

Boiled Bacon with Parsley Sauce and Split-Pea Soup

Serves 6

2 lb piece of smoked collar or forehock
$\frac{1}{2}$ lb split peas
4 oz onions (coarsely chopped)
2 cloves
1 carrot (sliced)
2 sticks celery (chopped)
1 leek (sliced)
1 bay leaf
1 oz flour
1 oz home-produced butter
$\frac{3}{4}$ pint milk
2 tablespoons parsley (chopped)
Salt and pepper

1 Cover the bacon with cold water and soak overnight.
Soak the split peas overnight.
2 Remove bacon joint from water. Calculate cooking
time, to allow 20 minutes to the pound, plus 20 minutes.
(If the joint is exactly 2 lb, it will therefore be 1 hour.)
3 Place joint in a saucepan with the drained split peas,
onions, cloves, carrot, celery, leek and bay leaf.
Slowly bring to the boil, then simmer gently for the
calculated time.
4 Place the flour, butter and milk in a saucepan, heat,
whisking continuously, until the sauce thickens.
Stir the chopped parsley into the sauce. Season
to taste.
5 Remove bacon from cooking liquid; cut away skin.
Carve joint into fairly thick slices on to warm plates.
Serve with parsley sauce—good with boiled potatoes
and carrots.
6 To finish the soup, continue cooking peas and stock
for another hour. Remove bay leaf, and cloves, then
sieve or liquidise soup. Reheat the soup when required,
adding a little of the chopped left-over bacon and a
spoonful of cream to each portion before serving.

Any recipe that gives two dishes for the time and
price of one is a real winner. The soup can be poured
into plastic containers and frozen to serve at a time
when bacon hasn't recently been on the menu!

Chinese Sweet and Sour Pork

Serves 6

2 lb belly pork
1 egg (beaten)
4 oz flour
$\frac{1}{4}$ pint milk
1 (7 oz) can pineapple cubes
2 oz onions (finely chopped)
1 oz home-produced butter
1 level tablespoon cornflour
2 level tablespoons brown sugar
1 clove garlic (finely chopped) optional
4 tablespoons vinegar
4 small tomatoes (quartered)
8 thick slices cucumber (diced)
1 piece stem ginger (finely chopped)
Salt and pepper
Deep fat for frying
9 oz long-grain rice (cooked)

1 Cut the rind and small bones away from pork. Cut the flesh into 1-inch squares. Fry the pork (without adding fat) over a low heat until the fat starts to run, then increase heat and fry quickly to brown.
2 Blend the beaten egg with the flour and milk to make a thick batter.
3 Strain the juice from the pineapple, making it up to $\frac{1}{2}$ pint with water.
4 Gently fry the onions in the butter until tender. Stir in the cornflour, brown sugar, garlic and vinegar. Blend in the pineapple juice and stir over a low heat until sauce thickens. Add the tomatoes, cucumber, ginger and pineapple cubes, then gently simmer the sauce. Season to taste.
5 Dip pork cubes in the batter and fry in preheated deep fat until crisp and golden.
6 Serve the crisp pork balls on a bed of plain boiled rice. Spoon over the hot sauce.
　　Cubes of fish dipped in the batter and fried are also good with sweet and sour sauce.

Cheshire Lamb Crumble

Serves 4

$\frac{3}{4}$ lb cold roast lamb
3 oz onions
$4\frac{1}{2}$ oz flour
1 level tablespoon tomato purée
$\frac{1}{2}$ pint stock
Salt and pepper
2 oz home-produced butter
2 oz Cheshire cheese (grated)
$\frac{1}{2}$ level teaspoon dried mixed herbs

1 Preheat the oven, mark 5, 375°F.
2 Mince together the meat and onions. Mix in $\frac{1}{2}$ oz of the flour, tomato purée, stock, salt and pepper. Turn into a pie dish.
3 Rub the butter into the remaining flour until it resembles fine breadcrumbs, then stir in the grated cheese, herbs, salt and pepper. Spoon the crumble over the meat. Bake for 45 minutes to 1 hour.

A good way of using left-over cold roast lamb—serve with baked tomatoes and mushrooms.

Canneloni

Serves 4

4 oz onions
2 tablespoons cooking oil
$\frac{1}{2}$ teaspoon mixed herbs
8-12 oz minced beef
1 (7 oz) can tomatoes
1 clove garlic (finely chopped or crushed) optional
4 oz mushrooms (sliced)
1 bay leaf
1 rounded teaspoon tomato purée
$\frac{1}{4}$ pint stock
Salt and pepper
8 squares of canneloni
   (or $\frac{1}{2}$ pint batter to make 8 small pancakes)
1 oz flour
1 oz home-produced butter
2 oz Scottish Cheddar cheese (grated)
$\frac{1}{2}$ pint milk

1 Finely chop 2 oz of the onions and fry in the oil with mixed herbs, over a high heat until dark brown.
Reduce heat and add the meat. Continue to cook for 5 minutes.
2 Add the tomatoes, garlic, mushrooms, remaining onions (sliced), bay leaf, tomato purée, stock, salt and pepper. Cover pan and cook very slowly for 30-40 minutes.
3 Either, cook the pasta as directed on the pack, and leave in cold water to cool, or
make the batter—smoothly blend 4 oz flour with 1 beaten egg and $\frac{1}{2}$ pint milk. Fry 8 pancakes.
4 Divide the meat mixture between 8 pasta squares or the pancakes. Roll them up and place in a heat-proof dish.
5 Place the flour, butter, grated cheese and milk in a saucepan. Whisk together over a low heat until sauce thickens. Season to taste.
6 Pour the cheese sauce over the stuffed canneloni. Bake—mark 5, 375°F, for 25-30 minutes.

Kebabs
with Barbecue Sauce

Serves 4

1 oz onions (very finely chopped)
1½ oz home-produced butter
1 tablespoon Worcestershire sauce
2 rounded tablespoons tomato ketchup
1 clove of garlic (very finely chopped) or garlic salt
1 tablespoon lemon juice
1 tablespoon demerara sugar
1 (5 fl oz) carton natural yogurt
Salt and pepper
¾ lb lean shoulder of lamb
1 lb chipolata sausages
8 shallots or baby onions
8 mushrooms
4 small tomatoes (halved)
6-8 oz long-grain rice (cooked)

1 Gently fry the chopped onions in the butter until
tender and turning brown. Remove pan from heat and
stir in the Worcestershire sauce, tomato ketchup,
garlic, lemon juice, sugar and yogurt. Season sauce to
taste with salt and pepper.
2 Cut the lamb into bite-size pieces. Twist the
sausages in half.
3 Blanch the shallots in boiling, salted water.
4 Pierce the pieces of meat and vegetables on to kebab
sticks or skewers.
5 Preheat the grill. Brush the kebabs liberally with the
barbecue sauce. Cook, turning frequently under
the hot grill.
6 Gently heat the sauce, do not allow it to boil.
7 Serve the kebabs on cooked rice with the sauce
served separately.

This is a hot spicy sauce for those who like really
flavourful dishes. It transforms almost any meat, but
is particularly good spooned over grilled hamburgers.

Italian Liver

Serves 4

$\frac{3}{4}$ lb ox or lamb's liver
$\frac{1}{2}$ pint milk
1 oz flour
Salt and pepper
$1\frac{1}{2}$ oz home-produced butter
1 lb onions (thinly sliced)
$\frac{1}{4}$ pint stock
2 level tablespoons tomato purée
1 clove garlic (finely chopped)
$\frac{1}{4}$ level teaspoon mixed dried herbs
2 tablespoons fresh cream
Chopped parsley

1 Cut liver into 1-inch pieces and soak in milk for 1 hour.
2 Remove the liver and coat in seasoned flour. Melt the butter in a frying pan and add the liver. Brown on all sides, then remove from pan.
3 Fry the onions slowly until tender. Gradually stir in the stock, milk, tomato purée, garlic and herbs. Bring sauce to the boil, stirring continuously.
4 Add the liver to the sauce. Cover pan and cook gently for 10-15 minutes until the liver is tender. Adjust seasoning to taste.
5 Place liver and sauce on a hot serving dish. Trickle cream over the liver and dust with chopped parsley.

A good variation to Italian Liver is—Russian Liver: fry 4 oz sliced mushrooms with the onions. Leave out the herbs and trickle over cream soured with a teaspoon of lemon juice. Both versions are good served with boiled spaghetti and courgettes, if available.

Courgettes—known as Zucchini in Italy—are a variety of small marrow. They are cooked unpeeled, either whole or sliced, in boiling water for 15-20 minutes. Cooked courgettes make a delicious salad when served cold, marinated in French dressing.

Moussaka

Serves 6

1½ lb potatoes (peeled and sliced)
3 tablespoons cooking oil
4 oz home-produced butter
4 oz onions (sliced)
1 clove garlic (finely chopped)
1 lb cooked lamb (chopped into small pieces)
1 (14 oz) can tomatoes
Salt and pepper
1 oz flour
½ pint milk
4 oz Scottish Cheddar cheese (grated)

1 Preheat the oven, mark 5, 375°F.
2 Fry the potatoes until soft in the oil and 3 oz of butter. Remove from the pan.
3 Add the onion slices and fry until soft, then add the finely chopped garlic, lamb, tomatoes and juice from the can. Mix together and season well with salt and pepper.
4 Line a buttered, shallow 2½–3-pint pie dish (or medium-size roasting pan) with the potatoes. Spread with the meat mixture.
5 Place the flour, 1 oz butter, milk, 2 oz of the grated cheese, salt and pepper in a saucepan. Heat, whisking continuously, until the sauce thickens.
6 Pour the sauce over the meat mixture. Sprinkle top with remaining grated cheese. Bake for about 30 minutes until top is golden brown.

This is a meal in itself and, at the most, requires just a green salad or cooked green vegetables served with it. An excellent way of using left-over roast lamb.

If aubergines are available cheaply, they are really nicer (and more correct) than potatoes. Slice them (without peeling). Fry (at stage 2) then use them to line the dish.

Savoury Meat Loaf

Serves 4

6 oz streaky bacon
8 oz cooked meat (minced)
$1\frac{1}{2}$ oz packet bread sauce mix
$\frac{1}{2}$ oz cornflakes (crumbled)
1 oz onions (chopped)
$\frac{1}{2}$ teaspoon mixed herbs
1 tablespoon tomato purée
1 egg
$\frac{1}{4}$ pint milk
Salt and pepper

1 Butter a 5-inch cake or 1-lb loaf tin and line with rashers of rindless streaky bacon.
2 Mix together the minced meat, bread sauce mix, cornflake crumbs, onions, herbs and tomato purée.
3 Beat the egg, add the milk and seasoning and stir into meat mixture. Beat well.
4 Turn into prepared tin, cover with aluminium foil.
5 Bake — mark 6, 400°F, for 1-$1\frac{1}{4}$ hours.
6 Turn out and serve hot with vegetables.
  Good served cold with salad too.

This is an excellent dish for using up the remains of the weekend joint. It can be prepared in advance and stored in the refrigerator until required, or wrapped in foil and frozen if you have a home freezer.

Fritto Misto

Serves 4

4 oz plain flour
Salt
3 tablespoons home-produced butter (melted)
$\frac{1}{4}$ pint milk (tepid)
Deep fat for frying
1 chicken breast
4 oz chicken livers
4 oz Scottish Cheddar cheese
Few flowerlets of cauliflower
$\frac{1}{2}$ lb courgettes
4 oz button mushrooms
4 oz prawns (peeled)
1 egg white
Lemon wedges

1 Mix the flour and salt with the melted butter.
Gradually blend in the tepid milk to make a smooth
coating batter.
2 Slowly heat the deep fat.
3 Cut the chicken flesh, chicken livers, cheese,
cauliflower and courgettes into thin bite-size pieces.
Place aside with the mushrooms and prawns.
4 Whisk the egg white very stiffly and fold into the batter.
5 Dip the prepared foods into the batter, then deep
fry them until crisp and golden. Drain.
6 Pile the Fritto Misto on to individual plates with
good-size lemon wedges.

This is one of my favourite Italian dishes—delicious
morsels in the crispest of batters. But the table must
be laid and people sitting and waiting for it. If the
Fritto Misto is kept waiting, it's ruined!

Instead of lemon (or as well as) Fritto Misto is good
with spicy Tartare Sauce (see page 16) or
Hollandaise Sauce.

Timewise tip: If you have a liquidiser, here is a
speedy recipe for Hollandaise Sauce.
Place 2 egg yolks in the liquidiser with 2 tablespoons
vinegar, 1 tablespoon lemon juice, salt and pepper.
Blend together, with liquidiser set at fastest speed.
Slowly pour in 3-4 oz melted home-produced
butter to make a thick, fluffy sauce. Stand sauce in a
bowl over hot water until required.

LIGHT LUNCHES AND SUPPER DISHES

1. & 2. Hamburgers with Hungarian Sauce—Page 72
3. Stilton Stuffed Eggs—Page 53
4. Chopped Pork and Ham Supper—Page 63
5. Piperade with Grilled Bacon—Page 57
6. Russian Meat Balls—Page 71

Cox's Cheese and Nut Toastie

Serves 4

3 Cox's apples
Juice ½ lemon
8 oz Scottish Cheddar cheese (grated)
Few drops Worcestershire sauce
4 slices bread
2 oz home-produced butter
1 oz walnuts (chopped)

1 Remove core from apples and cut one unpeeled apple into 8 thin rings. Dip in lemon juice. Peel and grate the other two apples.
2 Mix the cheese and grated apple with Worcestershire sauce.
3 Toast the bread on both sides and butter.
4 Spread the cheese mixture on to the toast and sprinkle top with chopped nuts.
5 Grill for 3-4 minutes until golden brown.
6 Garnish each toastie with two apple rings.

Stilton Stuffed Eggs

Serves 4

4 eggs (hard boiled)
2 oz White Stilton cheese (crumbled)
2 tablespoons fresh cream
Salt and pepper
Paprika
4 oz green beans (cooked)
2 tomatoes (sliced)
2 oz mushrooms
1 lettuce

1 Halve eggs lengthwise, remove yolks and mash with the cheese, cream, salt and pepper.
2 Pile back into egg halves. Sprinkle each with paprika. Serve on a tossed salad of cold cooked green beans, tomatoes, raw sliced mushrooms and lettuce.

Stuffed Omelette

Serves 1

1 oz watercress (finely chopped)
1 oz cream cheese
1 tablespoon fresh cream
Pepper
2 eggs
2 teaspoons milk
Salt
1 oz home-produced butter
Watercress

1 Mix watercress with cream cheese, cream and a little pepper.
2 Beat eggs, milk, salt and pepper lightly together with a fork.
3 Melt butter in a small frying pan over a fairly high heat. As soon as it is frothy (and before it browns) pour in eggs. Lightly fork to the centre of the pan until all the mixture has set underneath, while the top remains slightly runny. Remove from heat.
4 Spoon filling in centre and fold omelette over. Turn on to a warm plate, garnish with watercress and serve immediately.

Spanish Omelette

Serves 4

2-3 oz green pepper (core and seeds removed) optional
Salt
2 oz home-produced butter
1 lb potatoes (peeled and diced)
$\frac{1}{2}$ lb onions (diced)
4 eggs
4 tablespoons milk
Pepper
4 oz Scottish Cheddar cheese (grated)
Chopped parsley

1 Chop green pepper into small pieces and cook for
5 minutes in boiling salted water. Drain.
2 Melt the butter in a large frying pan. Add the diced
potatoes and onions and cook very slowly, turning
them from time to time until almost cooked through.
3 Beat the eggs, milk, salt and pepper together with a
fork.
4 Raise the heat under the frying pan; add the blanched
green pepper and continue cooking until the
vegetables are starting to brown.
5 Pour the omelette mixture over the vegetables,
stirring once or twice to allow it to spread evenly.
Leave pan until omelette starts to set and the
underside is turning golden.
6 Preheat the grill.
7 Scatter grated cheese over the omelette and pop the
pan under the grill until the cheese is bubbling and
turning golden brown.
8 Sprinkle the top of the omelette with parsley, cut it
into wedges and serve straight from the pan.

A delicious and surprisingly filling lunch or supper—
almost any vegetable can be diced and cooked (stage 2).
For a change try adding a mixture of chopped bacon,
sweetcorn and carrots.

Winter Salad

Serves 4

4 oz streaky bacon
1 head of chicory (if available)
4 sticks of celery
1 (7 oz) can sweetcorn (drained)
3 oz salted peanuts
4 oz ham (diced)
1 (5 fl oz) carton natural yogurt
1 tablespoon lemon juice
Salt and pepper

1 Remove rinds. Chop bacon and fry until crisp.
Leave aside until cold.
2 Cut the chicory into rings (using a stainless steel
knife to avoid discolouring) and chop the celery.
Place in a salad bowl.
3 Add the sweetcorn, peanuts, bacon and ham to the
salad bowl.
4 Just before serving, stir into the salad the yogurt,
lemon juice and plenty of salt and pepper. Toss well
together.

Pipérade
with Grilled Bacon

Serves 6

2 green peppers (core and seeds removed)
3 oz home-produced butter
6 oz onions (thinly sliced)
1 clove garlic (finely chopped or crushed) optional
1 lb tomatoes (skinned)
Salt and pepper
6 streaky bacon rashers
6 eggs
$\frac{1}{8}$ pint milk
Chopped parsley
Toast

1 Finely shred the green peppers and blanch in boiling salted water for 3 minutes. Drain.
2 Melt the butter in a large heavy saucepan and gently fry the onions, without browning. Remove seeds from tomatoes and chop. Add the blanched green peppers, garlic, chopped tomatoes, salt and pepper. Cover pan and cook very gently for 20 minutes.
3 Place the bacon rashers to cook under a low grill.
4 Lightly beat the eggs with the milk and pour on to the cooked vegetables. Stir, with a wooden spoon, over a medium heat until eggs are set. Season to taste.
5 Spoon the Pipérade on to hot dishes, top with the bacon rashers and a sprinkling of parsley. Serve with toast fingers.

Cheese and Egg Footballs

Serves 4-8

1½ lb potatoes (peeled)
2 oz home-produced butter
4 oz Scottish Cheddar cheese (grated)
1 tablespoon milk
Salt and pepper
5 eggs (hard boiled)
2 rounded teaspoons spring onion or onions
    (finely chopped)
1 egg (beaten)
Golden crumbs
Deep fat for frying

1 Cook the potatoes until soft. Drain well and mash
with the butter, cheese, milk, salt and pepper.
2 Chop the hard-boiled eggs coarsely and stir into the
potato with the chopped onions.
3 Divide the egg and potato mixture into 8 equal
portions, then roll into rounds. Brush with beaten egg,
then coat in golden crumbs.
4 Fry the 'footballs' in hot deep fat until crisp and
golden. Drain thoroughly.
   Try dividing the mixture into 16 equal portions, to
make Cheese and Egg Croquettes. Good served with a
crisp salad.

Janssen's Temptation

Serves 2-3

$\frac{3}{4}$ lb potatoes (thinly sliced)
$\frac{1}{2}$ lb onions (thinly sliced)
1 (2 oz) can anchovy fillets (finely chopped)
3 oz home-produced butter
$1\frac{1}{2}$ oz fresh white breadcrumbs
$\frac{1}{4}$ pint milk
2 oz Scottish Cheddar cheese (finely grated)

1 Preheat the oven, mark 6, 400°F.
2 Mix the potatoes with the onions, finely chopped anchovies and oil.
3 Turn potato mixture into a heatproof dish, thickly brushed with $1\frac{1}{2}$ oz butter.
4 Melt the remaining butter slowly and turn the breadcrumbs in it so they are well coated. Sprinkle them over the potatoes.
5 Cover dish with foil and bake for 35 minutes.
6 Remove foil from potatoes and pour the milk in at one side. Sprinkle with the cheese. Bake uncovered for a further 20-30 minutes until the potatoes are cooked and the crumbs golden brown.

A delicious Swedish dish that makes a warming snack for a winter evening, or a more substantial meal topped with fried eggs and bacon.

Findon Pancakes

Serves 4-8

1 egg (beaten)
6 oz flour
$1\frac{1}{2}$-$1\frac{3}{4}$ pints milk
2-3 oz home-produced butter
8 oz Finnan haddock (smoked)
Salt and pepper
2 eggs (hard boiled)
1 (1 oz) packet potato crisps (crushed)

1 Stir the beaten egg with 4 oz flour. Gradually blend in $\frac{1}{2}$ pint milk to form a smooth batter.
2 Heat a little butter in a frying pan. When the butter is hot, pour in sufficient batter to *thinly* coat the bottom of the pan. Brown one side, then turn and brown other side. Remove pancake from pan.
3 Use batter to make 8 pancakes in all.
4 Cook the haddock very gently in $\frac{1}{2}$ pint milk until tender.
5 Lift the cooked fish on to a plate with a draining spoon, flake.
6 Make the fish liquor up to 1 pint with the remaining cold milk. Place 2 oz flour, 2 oz butter and the fish liquor in a saucepan. Heat, whisking continuously, until sauce thickens.
7 Stir fish into half the sauce. Season to taste. Divide this filling between the 8 pancakes. Roll the pancakes up and arrange them in a rectangular heatproof dish.
8 Stir the chopped, hard-boiled eggs into the remaining sauce. Season to taste with salt and pepper, and spread over the stuffed pancakes. Sprinkle top with crushed crisps. Bake—mark 5, 375°F, for 15-20 minutes.

Cheese, Bacon and Pineapple Flan

Serves 4

6 oz plain flour
Salt
3 oz home-produced butter
3 oz bacon rashers
1 (7 oz) can pineapple cubes
2 eggs
1 (8 oz) carton cottage cheese
Pepper
1 level tablespoon mixed mustard
2 tomatoes (sliced)

1 Sieve the flour with a pinch of salt. Rub in the butter until the mixture resembles fine breadcrumbs. Bind together with a little water to make a firm dough.
2 Roll the pastry out to line a 7—8-inch flan ring or sandwich tin.
3 Remove rinds and chop the bacon into bite-size pieces. Drain the pineapple.
4 Beat the eggs in a bowl, stir in the cottage cheese, bacon, pineapple, salt, pepper and mustard. Pour filling into pastry case.
5 Bake—mark 4, 350°F, for 40-50 minutes. Serve hot or cold, garnished with sliced tomatoes.

Chopped Pork and Ham Supper

Serves 4

3 oz quick cooking macaroni
3 oz onions (sliced)
$1\frac{1}{2}$ oz home-produced butter
1 oz flour
$\frac{1}{2}$ pint milk
1 rounded tablespoon tomato purée
Salt and pepper
1 ($7\frac{1}{2}$ oz) can chopped pork and ham or luncheon meat
3 oz Scottish Cheddar cheese (grated)
2 tomatoes (sliced)

1 Cook the macaroni in boiling salted water for
8 minutes (or as directed on the pack).
2 Slowly fry the onions in $\frac{1}{2}$ oz of the butter until tender.
Add the drained macaroni.
3 Place the remaining 1 oz of butter, flour and milk in a
saucepan, heat, whisking continuously until the sauce
thickens. Stir in tomato purée, salt and pepper to taste.
4 Dice the meat. Stir it into the onions and macaroni
together with the sauce and 2 oz of the grated cheese.
Turn into a shallow $1\frac{1}{2}$-pint pie dish.
5 Arrange the sliced tomatoes over the top of the pie
and sprinkle with remaining cheese. Bake—mark 5,
375°F for 25 minutes.

It is a good idea to always keep the ingredients for
this quick and easy supper dish in the store cupboard.
For a change, chopped bacon or ham can replace the
canned meat.
Timewise tip: For a quick, unusual, light savoury dish
try tossing some cooked spaghetti in a little heated
cream, well seasoned with salt and pepper and a pinch
of mixed herbs. Serve sprinkled with Scottish Cheddar
cheese.

Ham
with Florida Coleslaw

Serves 4

1 lb small white cabbage (finely shredded)
2 dessert apples (peeled and grated)
2 medium carrots (peeled and grated)
2 oz raisins
1 oz onions (very finely chopped)
1 orange
1 (5 fl oz) carton natural yogurt
2 rounded tablespoons mayonnaise
1 dessertspoon lemon juice
Salt and pepper
$\frac{1}{2}$-$\frac{3}{4}$ lb cooked ham

1 Combine the shredded cabbage with the grated
apple and carrot, raisins, onions, finely grated rind and
juice from half the orange.
2 Stir the yogurt, mayonnaise, lemon juice and plenty
of salt and pepper into the vegetables. Toss well
together. Turn into a salad dish and garnish with slices
cut from the remaining orange half.
   Serve the Florida Coleslaw with thick slices of ham—
or good, too, with tuna fish.

Note: Salad cream may be used instead of
mayonnaise, but it does make a thinner dressing.
Alternatively, the coleslaw can be tossed in the dressing
without the mayonnaise being added—it is then
excellent for slimmers.

Ham and Pineapple Topnots

Serves 4

4 rounds ham steaks or 4 (2 oz) pieces cooked ham
4 crumpets or rounds of bread
4 oz Scottish Cheddar cheese (grated)
$\frac{1}{2}$ level teaspoon mustard powder
4 dessertspoons milk
4 pineapple rings
Watercress

1 Slowly grill the ham steaks. Toast the crumpets at the same time.
2 Mix the cheese, mustard and milk together to form a paste. Spread the paste on top of each toasted crumpet and grill until golden brown.
3 Place the grilled ham steaks on top of the toasted cheese and crown with the rings of pineapple. Heat through under the grill. Top with sprigs of watercress.

   The combination of the fruit with the hot cheese is delicious. Try peach or pear halves instead as a change.

Soufflé Rarebit

Serves 4

4 slices of bread (crusts removed)
4 oz Caerphilly cheese
4 eggs (separated)
4 teaspoons milk
Salt and pepper

1 Preheat the oven, mark 4, 350°F.
2 Toast the slices of bread on one side.
3 Slice the Caerphilly cheese, and place on the
untoasted sides of the bread.
4 Beat the egg yolks with the milk, salt and pepper.
5 Whisk the egg whites until very stiff, then fold the
egg yolks into them. Pile on top of the slices.
6 Bake for 10-15 minutes until well risen and golden
brown. Serve immediately.

Stilton Soufflé

Serves 4

3 oz home-produced butter
2 oz flour
Salt and pepper
$\frac{1}{2}$ level teaspoon mustard powder
4 oz White Stilton cheese (crumbled)
$\frac{1}{2}$ pint milk
3 large eggs

1 Preheat the oven, mark 6, 400°F.
2 Place the butter, flour, salt, pepper, mustard, cheese
and milk in a heavy saucepan.
3 Stand the saucepan over a low heat and stir
continuously until sauce comes to the boil and thickens.
4 Separate the eggs. Whisk the whites until very stiff.
5 Beat the egg yolks into the sauce, then carefully fold
in the whisked whites until well blended.
6 Turn soufflé into a buttered (No. 2) 2-pint soufflé
dish and cook for 35-40 minutes until well risen.
   Serve with a mixed salad.

   Soufflés are eggs added to a flavoured white sauce.
They are extremely simple to make and foolproof,
provided the whites are really whisked until peaky.

Onion Tart (Tarte à l'Oignon)

Serves 6

1½ lb large onions
3½ oz home-produced butter
1½ oz lard
7 oz flour
3 eggs
8 fl oz milk
Salt and pepper

1 Slice the onions very thinly. Melt 1½ oz of the butter in a heavy saucepan. Add the onions, cover and cook very slowly until they start to soften.
2 Rub the remaining 2 oz of butter and lard into the flour, then bind together with a little water to form a firm dough.
3 Roll the pastry out to line an 8–9-inch flan or sandwich tin.
4 Beat eggs with the milk, salt and pepper. Add the onions and turn mixture into the pastry case. Bake— mark 7, 425°F, for 35-40 minutes, until the pastry is cooked and the filling set with a golden-brown top.
    Serve hot or cold.

Spanish Potato Balls with Bacon (Noquis Con Jamon)

Serves 4

(pronounced Ne-o-kis)

1½ lb potatoes
5½ oz flour
2 eggs (beaten)
Salt and pepper
3 oz home-produced butter
3 oz Scottish Cheddar cheese (grated)
¾ pint milk
8 rashers bacon
4 tomatoes (skinned)
2 teaspoons onions (very finely chopped)
Chopped parsley

1 Preheat the oven, mark 8, 450°F.
2 Boil the potatoes in their skins. When cooked, peel them and rub through a sieve. Add 4 oz of the flour, beaten eggs, salt and pepper. Mix well to a stiff dough.
3 Roll the potato dough on a floured board into balls the size of a hazelnut. Cook them for 3 minutes in plenty of boiling salted water (probably best done in 3 batches).
4 Lift the potato balls out with a draining spoon and spread them in a shallow baking dish, thickly greased with 1½ oz butter.
5 Place the remaining 1½ oz of flour, butter, grated cheese and milk in a saucepan. Whisk together over a low heat until sauce thickens. Season to taste. Pour over the potato balls. Bake for 5-10 minutes.
6 Remove rind from bacon, then roll rashers around tomatoes to completely cover. Spear them on to kebab sticks or skewers.
7 Place kebabs on top of the potato balls and cook for a further 5-10 minutes until bacon is crisp and tomatoes are cooked. Serve the dish sprinkled with onion and parsley

A dish that is different. The baked potato balls are also good served with sausages or cold sliced meat instead of the bacon kebabs.

Quick Sausage Stroganoff

Serves 4

1 lb beef sausages
4 oz onions (sliced)
4 oz pasta noodles
1 oz home-produced butter
1 (10 oz) can condensed mushroom soup
2 teaspoons vinegar
$\frac{1}{4}$ pint milk
Salt and pepper
Chopped chives
2 medium-cooked beetroots (sliced)
Whipped cream (optional)

1 Cut each sausage into 4 pieces. Fry gently with the sliced onions until cooked through and golden brown.
2 Boil the noodles for 8 minutes (or as directed on the pack), drain. Toss in butter and spoon round the edge of a serving dish. Cover with foil and keep warm.
3 Add the soup, vinegar and milk to the sausages and onions. Cook together until bubbling. Season to taste, then pour into the centre of the noodles. Sprinkle with chopped chives.
4 Arrange slices of beetroot and spoonfuls of whipped cream sprinkled with chopped chives on the noodles.

For Drinks Party. ✳
Serve small with c. sticks ✳

Russian Meat Balls (Bitkis)

Serves 4

4 oz sliced bread
Milk
4 oz onions (finely chopped)
$\frac{3}{4}$ lb veal (minced)
Salt and pepper
2 oz home-produced butter
6 oz mushrooms (sliced)
1 oz flour
1 (14 oz) can tomatoes
1 tablespoon lemon juice
1 stock cube
$\frac{1}{4}$ pint water
1 level teaspoon sugar
1 rounded teaspoon tomato purée
2-3 tablespoons soured cream
Chopped parsley

1 Remove crusts from bread. Place slices in a shallow dish and just cover with milk.
2 Mix the chopped onions with the minced veal. Season with salt and pepper.
3 Squeeze the bread, and fork it into the meat. Knead the mixture together, then divide into 12 equal parts and roll into balls on a well-floured board.
4 Fry the meat balls in half the butter until well browned on all sides. Lift them out with a draining spoon into a heatproof dish.
5 Fry the mushrooms in the frying pan with remaining butter. Lift them out with a draining spoon into the dish with the meat balls.
6 Add to the buttery pan juices, flour, tomatoes, lemon juice, stock cube, water, sugar, tomato purée, salt and pepper. Whisk over a medium heat until sauce thickens.
7 Sieve (or liquidise) the tomato sauce and pour it over the meat balls and mushrooms. Bake—mark 4 350°F, for 35-40 minutes.
8 Just before serving, spoon the soured cream over the meat balls and sprinkle with chopped parsley.
   Serve with a tossed green salad.

Hamburgers
with Hungarian Sauce

Serves 4

$\frac{3}{4}$ lb minced beef
Salt and pepper
3 oz onions (finely chopped)
3 oz home-produced butter
$\frac{1}{2}$ lb onions (sliced)
4 oz button mushrooms (sliced)
1 oz flour
2 level tablespoons paprika
1 (7 oz) can tomatoes
2 tablespoons tomato purée
1 tablespoon lemon juice
$\frac{1}{2}$ pint stock
Salt and pepper
4 tablespoons soured cream

1 Mix the minced meat, salt and pepper with the chopped onion. Divide into 4 and shape into round flat hamburgers. Place hamburgers in a shallow heatproof dish. Grill for 10 minutes on each side. Keep hot.
2 Melt the butter. Fry the sliced onions and then the mushrooms. When tender remove from pan with a draining spoon. Keep hot.
3 Stir into the pan juices, the flour, paprika, tomatoes, tomato purée, lemon juice, stock, salt and pepper. Keep stirring over a low heat until sauce thickens. Return onions and mushrooms to pan. Check seasoning.
4 Add soured cream to the sauce. Mix thoroughly.
5 Serve hamburgers and hand sauce separately.
   Good served with plain boiled noodles.

PUDDINGS

Sugar Plum Pie

Serves 6

6 oz plain flour
$\frac{1}{4}$ level teaspoon salt
3 oz home-produced butter
2 level teaspoons caster sugar
4 egg yolks
Milk
$\frac{1}{2}$ oz granulated sugar
2 (5 fl oz) cartons natural yogurt
$\frac{1}{2}$ level teaspoon powdered cinnamon
1 lb dessert plums
1 oz blanched almonds (optional)
$1\frac{1}{2}$ oz demerara sugar

1 Sieve the flour with the salt into a bowl. Rub in the butter until it resembles fine breadcrumbs. Stir in caster sugar, then bind together with 1 egg yolk and milk to form a stiff dough.
2 Roll out dough to line an 8-inch pie plate or flat tin.
3 Beat 3 remaining egg yolks with granulated sugar, yogurt and cinnamon. Pour into pastry shell.
4 Cut plums in half. Remove stones, then arrange, cut side up, in yogurt custard.
5 Bake—mark 6, 400°F, for 35-40 minutes.
6 Preheat grill. Place an almond in the centre of each plum and sprinkle top of pie with demerara sugar. Grill until golden brown.

Coeur à la Crème

Serves 4

1 (8 oz) carton cottage cheese
1½ oz caster sugar
2 tablespoons fresh double cream
2 egg whites
Fresh strawberries or raspberries and sugar
1 (5 fl oz) carton fresh cream

1 Using a wooden spoon, press the cottage cheese through a sieve into a bowl. Mix in the sugar and cream.
2 Whisk the egg whites until very stiff, then fold into the cottage cheese mixture.
3 Spoon the cheese mixture into a serving dish and smooth over the top. Scatter with sugared strawberries or raspberries. Serve with cream.

A delicious hot summer's day dessert. Often made richer by folding in more double cream and then drained overnight in special heart-shaped moulds—hence its name.

Elizabeth's Cider Syllabub

Serves 3-4

1 (5 fl oz) carton fresh double cream
½ lemon (grated rind and juice)
2 oz caster sugar
½ wine glass (1½ fl oz) cider
Crisp shortbread fingers

1 Whip the cream until thick. Add finely grated rind and strained juice of lemon and the sugar.
2 Gradually blend in the cider. Spoon into 3-4 individual glasses. Chill in refrigerator or stand in cool place. Serve with shortbread or other crisp biscuits.

This is a delicious variation of our traditional Elizabethan syllabub. Even dishes using as much cream as this can be economical.
Whipping fresh cream: The bowl, the whisk and the cream itself must be really cold. The cream should be whipped quickly at first until it takes on a matt finish and then slowly, until it stands in smooth peaks.

Tutti-Frutti Whip

Serves 4-6

1 pint milk
1 (1 pint) packet instant dessert
2 oz desiccated coconut
2 oz glacé cherries (chopped)
1 oz angelica (chopped)
2 bananas (sliced)

1 Pour milk into a basin. Sprinkle on the instant dessert and whisk until thick.
2 Stir in nearly all the coconut, cherries, angelica and sliced bananas. Spoon into 4-6 individual dishes and sprinkle a little of the remaining coconut on top of each.

French Apple Flan

Serves 8

4 oz granulated sugar
1½ lb dessert apples (peeled, cored and thinly sliced)
1 (13 oz) packet frozen puff pastry (thawed)
1 egg
¾ pint milk
2½ oz caster sugar
1 oz flour
1 level teaspoon cornflour
1 level teaspoon arrowroot or cornflour
1 level teaspoon lemon rind (finely grated)

1 Preheat oven, mark 7, 425°F.
2 Dissolve the granulated sugar in ½ pint water over a low heat. Add the apples.
3 Roll the pastry out to a rectangle, trim to 12 inches × 9 inches. Place pastry on a moistened baking tray.
4 Beat the egg and use a little to brush over the surface of the pastry.
5 With a sharp knife, mark the pastry all round, 1 inch from the edge, to form a vol-au-vent case.
6 Bake for 25 minutes. When cooked, remove centre piece of pastry with a sharp knife.
7 Place the milk in a pan and heat slowly. Mix the caster sugar into the beaten egg, then stir in the flour and cornflour. When the milk is almost boiling, stir it by degrees into the egg mixture. Return to pan and, whisking continuously, heat slowly until the pastry cream is thick and creamy. Pour into the flan case.
8 Lift the poached apples out of the syrup with a draining spoon and arrange them decoratively over the pastry cream.
9 Gradually blend the apple syrup into the arrowroot (or cornflour), then add the lemon rind. Stir over a gentle heat until it comes to the boil. Continue boiling until glaze is clear, then spoon it over the apples. Leave aside until cold.

An excellent way of using up windfalls.

Princess Pudding

Serves 4-5

1 pint milk
1 oz home-produced butter
1 orange (finely grated rind and juice)
3 oz caster sugar
4 oz fresh breadcrumbs
2 eggs (separated)
3 tablespoons apricot jam

1 Slowly heat together the milk, butter, orange rind
and 1 oz of the sugar. Remove from heat. Add
breadcrumbs and place aside for 15 minutes.
2 Beat the egg yolks into the crumb mixture and pour
into a buttered 2-pint pie dish.
3 Bake—mark 3, 325°F, for about 40-45 minutes,
until cooked through and firm.
4 Combine apricot jam and orange juice. Spread over
pudding.
5 Whisk egg whites until very stiff. Fold in the
remaining caster sugar. Spread over jam and return to
oven for further 20-25 minutes until meringue is
crisp and golden brown.

To keep cream or milk without a refrigerator, stand
carton or bottle in a basin containing a little water.
Cover it with a clean cloth with its edges completely
immersed in the water. Evaporation of the water
keeps the products cool and fresh.

Honeyed Lemon Whip

Serves 2-3

1 (5 fl oz) carton natural yogurt
2 tablespoons clear honey or 1 oz caster sugar
½ lemon (peeled rind and juice)
1 egg white

1 Mix the yogurt with the honey or sugar and lemon juice.
2 Whisk the egg white until very stiff, then fold into the
yogurt and honey mixture.
3 Spoon the whip into 2-3 individual glasses and
decorate each with a curl of lemon rind.
4 Serve immediately.

Hot Swiss Trifle

Serves 4

1 swiss roll
1 (12½ oz) can apricots (drained)
2 tablespoons custard powder
2 eggs (separated)
1 tablespoon sugar
1 pint milk
4 oz caster sugar
1 oz blanched almonds (optional)

1 Slice the swiss roll and arrange with the apricots in a 1½-pint fireproof dish.
2 Blend the custard powder, egg yolks and sugar together with a little of the milk.
3 Heat the rest of the milk and when nearly boiling, stir on to the mixed custard.
4 Return to the pan and bring to the boil, stirring continuously and when thick, pour over the apricots.
5 Whisk the egg whites until stiff and fold in caster sugar.
6 Pile meringue on top of the custard and stud with blanched almonds.
7 Bake—mark 4, 350°F, for about 20 minutes.

Toffeed Rice

Serves 4

1 pint milk
4 oz caster sugar
1 oz home-produced butter
2 oz Carolina pudding rice
1 teaspoon vanilla essence
4 tablespoons fresh cream
1 oz stem ginger or
   2 oz candied peel (chopped)

1 Place the milk, 2 oz of the sugar, butter, rice and vanilla essence in a saucepan over a very low heat for at least 2 hours.
2 Cool the rice slightly, then stir in the cream, ginger or chopped peel. Pour rice into a 1-pint heatproof dish or 4 individual heatproof dishes. Chill well.
3 Heat the grill. Spread the remaining 2 oz of sugar over the rice and place as close as possible under the hot grill, until the sugar caramelises to a golden brown.
4 Chill the rice thoroughly before serving.

Pineapple
Cheesecake Pie

Serves 6

2 oz home-produced butter
4 oz plain flour
1 level teaspoon caster sugar
Pinch of salt
1 (4 oz) carton cottage cheese
1 oz home-produced butter (softened)
$3\frac{1}{2}$ oz caster sugar
1 egg (beaten)
1 oz flour
$\frac{1}{8}$ pint milk
2 slices pineapple (drained and chopped)
Whipped cream $\Big\}$ optional decoration
Pineapple

1 Rub butter into the flour, sugar and pinch of salt until mixture resembles fine breadcrumbs. Bind together with a little water to form a firm dough.
2 Roll pastry to fit a 6-inch flan or sandwich tin. Loosely line with foil and fill with baking beans. Bake—mark 6, 400°F, for 15 minutes.
3 Sieve cottage cheese. Mix in the soft butter, caster sugar, beaten egg, flour and milk.
4 After 15 minutes, remove flan from oven. Lift out foil and beans. Spread the chopped pineapple over the bottom of the flan and spoon over the cottage cheese mixture.
5 Bake flan for a further 20-30 minutes until filling has set. If liked, flan may be decorated with whirls of whipped cream and pieces of pineapple.

Cream care
   Cream should always be kept cool, and away from bright light or strong sunshine.
Ideally, it should be kept covered (film wrap or foil is good for this) in a refrigerator, and stored away from any food that might taint it. The best way to buy fresh cream is—a little and often.

Magic Lemon Pudding

Serves 4-6

1 large lemon (grated rind and juice)
2 oz home-produced butter
4 oz caster sugar
2 eggs (separated)
2 oz self-raising flour
½ pint milk

1 Preheat the oven, mark 4, 350°F.
2 Add the lemon rind to the butter and sugar. Cream together until soft.
3 Add the beaten egg yolks and a little flour. Stir in the milk, strained lemon juice and remaining sifted flour alternately.
4 Whisk the egg whites until stiff and fold in evenly.
5 Pour into a greased 1½-pint pie dish and bake for 40 minutes.
   This pudding cooks to give a light sponge top with a tangy lemon sauce underneath. Good served topped with sweetened whipped cream and a little grated lemon rind.

Orange Mousse

Serves 4-6

½ oz powdered gelatine
2 (5 fl oz) cartons natural yogurt
1 (6¼ oz) can frozen concentrated orange juice
   (unsweetened)
2 egg whites

1 Set refrigerator to coldest setting.
2 Place gelatine with 2 tablespoons of water in a cup. Stand the cup in very hot water until gelatine has dissolved.
3 Whisk the yogurt, thawed orange juice, and dissolved gelatine together.
4 Whisk the egg whites until very stiff, and as the yogurt mixture begins to set, fold whisked whites into it.
5 Pour mixture into a plastic container. Place in the refrigerator ice-box and freeze.
6 Spoon mousse into individual dishes for serving.
   A good dish for summer slimmers.

Buttered Apples

Serves 4-6

1½ lb dessert apples
3 oz home-produced butter
2-3 oz demerara sugar

1 Peel and thinly slice the apples.
2 Slowly melt the butter in a frying pan and add the fruit and sugar.
3 Gently shake the frying pan over a medium heat until the apple slices are cooked through.
4 Serve in individual dishes—hot or cold.
   Superb served with whipped cream to which a little finely grated orange or lemon rind has been added—and, on lush occasions, some orange liqueur.

   Handy tip: To remove wrapping from butter almost completely clean—first run the pack under cold water.

Lemon Meringue Tops

Serves 4-6

1 oz cornflour
½ pint milk
2 oz sugar
1 oz home-produced butter
1 lemon (grated rind and juice)
2 eggs (separated)
2 oz caster sugar

1 Blend cornflour with the milk. Stir mixture over medium heat until sauce is thick.
2 Add sugar, butter and lemon rind. Stir in lemon juice.
3 Cool slightly. Stir in egg yolks. Turn mixture into 4-6 individual oven-proof dishes.
4 Whisk the whites very stiffly. Fold in all but a teaspoon of the caster sugar. Pile meringue over the lemon filling in each dish. Sprinkle with remaining sugar. Bake—mark 6, 400°F, for 6-8 minutes until the meringue is golden brown.

Minted Meringue Ice

Serves 4-6

1¾ pints milk
8 oz granulated sugar
1 teaspoon peppermint essence
4 egg whites
2 oz plain dessert chocolate (coarsely chopped)
Sprigs of fresh mint

1 Set the ice-making compartment of your refrigerator to its coolest setting.
2 Heat the milk, sugar and peppermint essence very gently together to dissolve the sugar, then bring to the boil. Leave until cold.
3 Pour the cooled milk mixture into a suitable plastic container and place in ice compartment until semi-frozen.
4 Whisk the egg whites until very stiff.
5 Mush down the semi-frozen ice with a fork and fold in the whisked egg whites. Return to ice compartment until frozen.
6 Spoon the meringue ice into goblets and top with chopped chocolate and sprigs of mint.

An unusual summer dessert that will set your visitors or family talking. Use up the egg yolks to enrich mashed potato.

CHILDREN'S RECIPES

Dishes children like to eat ...and cook for themselves.

We can't live without food, and as so much of our time is spent preparing it we may as well encourage our children to grow up enjoying cooking—if they don't know a little about cooking, they won't appreciate food to its full.

As the children cook, they will learn about the value of food: how to make food look attractive; how to make the most out of food ... and that is really what being a penny-wise cook is about.

It is a good idea for someone to be nearby while children are cooking. Firstly to give encouragement (even if the end results are a little singed!) and secondly the kitchen is quite a hazardous room to be left in.

Some of the recipes are in heavy coloured type to indicate where a special watch should be made.

Children, before starting to cook, here are a few points that should always be remembered:

1 Read the recipe right through and make sure you know what you have to do. Ask someone to explain anything you do not understand.

2 Put on an apron, wash hands and lay the table (if this is necessary).

3 Wipe over the work-surface you will be working on.

4 Get out all equipment you need to make the recipe.

5 Check at what stage the oven should be lit; this will take about 15 minutes to heat up.

6 Measure all your ingredients carefully.

7 As you work, remove dirty dishes to a bowl of hot water, and keep work-surface well wiped.

8 Clear up the kitchen when you have finished; remember to do this well or you may not be so welcome in the kitchen next time!

Beany Pies.

SERVES 6

Ingredients
12 thin slices of bread (small loaf)
Butter for spreading
2 oz Scottish Cheddar cheese
1 (5 oz) can baked beans
3 tomatoes (cut in half)

Set oven—mark 6 (400F°)

Utensils
Bread board
Butter knife
Cheese grater
Plate
Patty tin or bun ti
Can opener
Dessert spoon
2-inch pastry cut
Oven glove
Knife
Serving plate

1 Remove the crusts from the bread, and spread quite thickly with butter.

2 Grate the cheese with a coarse grater.

3 Press 6 of the slices of bread, buttered side down, into 6 fairly deep patty or bun tins.

4 Open the can.

Divide the baked beans between the 6 lined tins.

Using a pastry cutter, cut the
remaining slices of bread into rounds
(to fit top of patty tins) and place
them buttered side up, on top of the
baked beans.

Sprinkle the grated
cheese on top of each pie.

7 Bake the pies towards the
top of the oven for 15-20
minutes. Place the tomatoes
in the oven for the last
5-10 minutes to bake.

Remove the pies from
the oven, lift them out of the
tins with a knife, and cool
slightly before serving.

Decorate with tomato halves on
top of each pie.

Pigs in a Poke.

SERVES 4

Ingredients
4 large potatoes for baking
4 pork sausages
4 oz Double Gloucester
  or Scottish Cheddar cheese
Salt and pepper
2 tablespoons milk
1 oz home-produced butter

Set oven—mark 5 (375F°)

Utensils
Vegetable brush
Fork
2 baking trays
Oven glove
Cheese grater
Plate
Mixing bowl
Potato masher
Dessert spoon
Knife
Serving plate

1 Scrub the potatoes in cold water, pat them dry and prick all over with a fork.

2 Put the potatoes on a baking tray and place in the centre of the oven. Cook for 1-1½ hours, until, when pressed lightly with an oven glove, they feel soft.

3 While the potatoes are cooking, place sausages in a tin, and cook in the oven for ¾ hour. Remove and keep hot.

4 Grate the cheese.

Remove potatoes from oven with an oven glove.
Cut them almost through lengthwise.
Carefully, without breaking
the skins, scoop out the hot
potato into a bowl.

Add the grated cheese,
salt, pepper, milk and
butter to the potato
and mash well.

Spoon a quarter of the mixture back into
each of the potato skins.

Place a sausage in the centre of each potato.

Serve immediately.

Orange Yogurt Flan.

SERVES 6

Ingredients
¼ pint milk
1 (½ pint packet) orange
   instant dessert
2 (6 fl oz) cartons orange yogurt
1 sponge flan case
Chocolate flake or few
   chocolate buttons

Utensils
2-pint mixing bowl
Measuring jug
Whisk
Tablespoon
Serving plate

1 Pour the milk into the
bowl and sprinkle on the
instant dessert powder.
2 Whisk the two together
           until thick.

3 Then whisk in
both yogurts.

4 Place the sponge flan case on
a serving plate and spoon
in the orange yogurt whip.

5 Decorate with
chocolate.

Raspberry & Lemon Cooler.

SERVES 2

Utensils
2-pint mixing bowl
Measuring jug
Whisk
Tablespoon
2 drinking glasses

Ingredients
1 (6 fl oz) carton raspberry
   flavour yogurt
¼ pint fizzy lemonade
2 tablespoons vanilla ice cream

1 Whisk the yogurt
and lemonade quickly
together in a bowl.

2 Place a spoonful of ice cream
in each glass.

3 Pour on the yogurt
and lemonade.

Serve immediately.

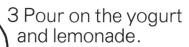

Minted Hot Chocolate Drink.

SERVES 3

Ingredients
3 rounded teaspoons
   drinking chocolate
4 peppermint cream sweets
   (crushed or crumbled)
1 pint milk

Utensils
Saucepan
Wooden spoon
2-pint mixing bowl
Whisk
Jug
3 mugs

1 Place the drinking
chocolate, peppermint
creams and milk
together in a saucepan.

2 Heat the milk very slowly to
boiling point, stirring from
time to time, until the
peppermint creams have
dissolved.

3 Remove from the heat.
Pour into a bowl and whisk.

4 Pour drink into 3 mugs.

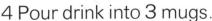